Handbook for
Anglo-Chromatic Concertina

by
Roger
Watson

Wise Publications
London/New York/Sydney/Cologne

GW00646354

£1.95

Wise Publications
London/New York/Sydney/Cologne

Exclusive Distributors:
Music Sales Ltd.
78 Newman Street, London W1P 3LA, England

Music Sales Pty Ltd.
27 Clarendon Street, Artarmon, Sydney, NSW 2064, Australia

Music Sales GmbH
Kolner Strasse 199, 5000 Cologne 90, West Germany

© Copyright 1981 Wise Publications

UK Order No AM 28325
ISBN 0 86001 852 0

Cover Design CleaverLandor
Book Design CleaverLandor
Photography Andrew Kimm

Music Sales' complete catalogue lists thousands of titles and
is free from your local music book shop, or direct from
Music Sales Limited. Please send 15p in stamps for postage
to Music Sales Limited, 78 Newman Street, London W1P 3LA.

Printed in England by JB Offset (Marks Tey) Limited
Marks Tey, Essex.

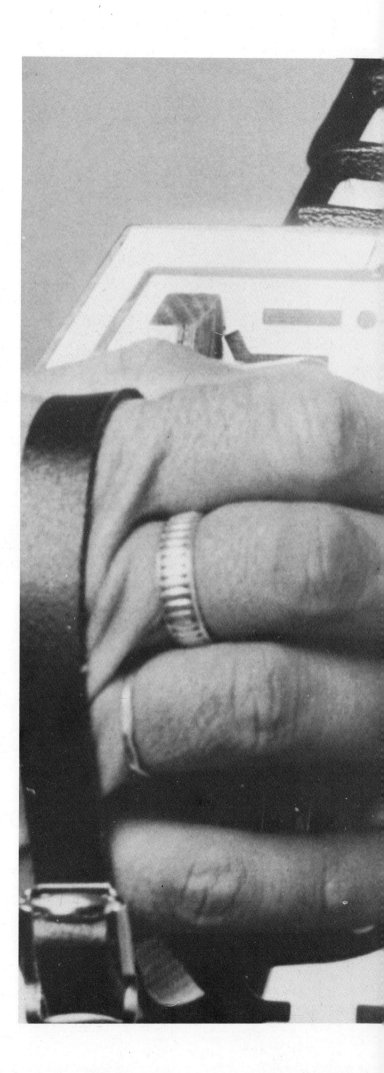

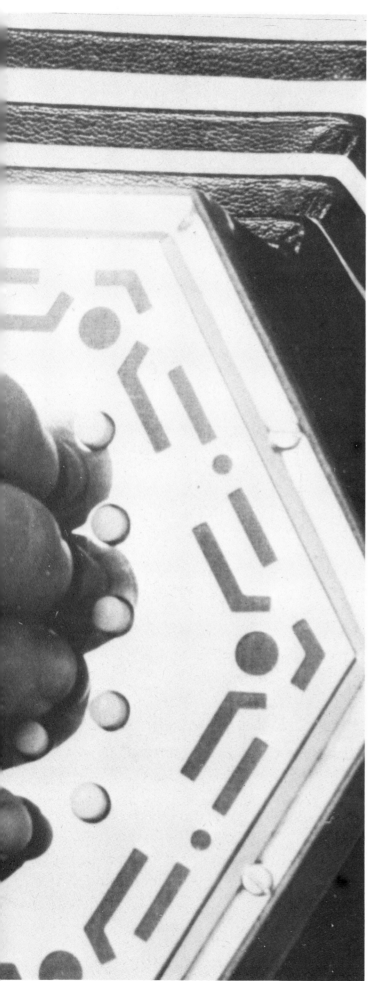

Contents

The Concertina and the Folk Music Revival

The concertina belongs to the family of 'free reed' instruments, that is, instruments which make their sound by the passage of air vibrating metal reeds. Other instruments of this type are the harmonica, accordion, melodeon and harmonium.

The English concertina was invented in 1829 by Sir Charles Wheatstone, who registered a patent on the instrument. Classical pieces were written for it, and its large and fully chromatic range makes it capable of playing music written for such instruments as the violin, clarinet and oboe. But its tone has never appealed greatly to those involved in orchestral music. Instead, Wheatstone's invention, along with its close cousin, the Anglo-Chromatic concertina,

became largely an instrument for 'popular' musicians.

The distinctive bellows action of the 'squeeze-box' has made the term 'concertina' almost universally known, to the extent that many do not take it seriously as an instrument. Yet, its versatility and portability led to its great popularity in the later 19th and in the 20th centuries. Travelling musicians and sailors found its compact size a great advantage; the Salvation Army made good use of its strident tone; concertina bands were popular in many towns particularly in the North; music hall performers demonstrated the extent of virtuosity which could be reached on the concertina. But the greatest and

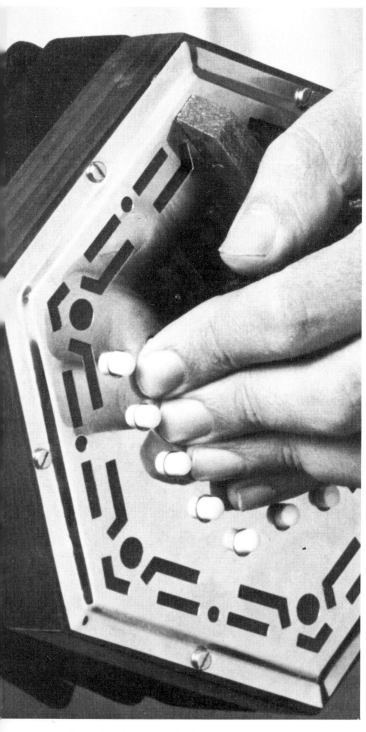

The English Concertina

most long-lasting popularity of the instrument, however, has been among singers and players of folk music.

There are two basic types of concertina. First, Wheatstone's English system, which plays the same note whether the bellows are pushed or pulled. It is fully chromatic, that is, it has all the sharps and flats necessary to play in all keys. An English concertina is recognizable by having four parallel straight rows of buttons on each end, thumb straps and little finger slides. Some English concertinas have wrist straps as well. The buttons for playing the lower notes are situated on the part of each end which is closer to the body when the instrument is

held in the normal playing position. Notable makers of the English system were Wheatstone himself, Lachenal, (an employee of Wheatstone who later formed an independent company) Jones and Crabbe. The firm of Crabbe are still producing a small number of instruments, and the Wheatstone company name has recently been revived, although production is, as yet, very small. Second, there is the Anglo-chromatic concertina ('Anglo' for short), which, like the harmonica and melodeon, also of Germanic origin, plays different notes when blown and sucked (that is, when the bellows are squeezed together or pulled apart). An Anglo concertina has wrist strap, and at least two rows of buttons arranged in an arc forward of straps. It has an air release button, usually correctly positioned for the right thumb. To be fully chromatic, an Anglo has to have a large number of buttons (with 30 or more, a number of keys are possible) as well as more variation within the basic keys of the two main rows. The lower notes are played by the buttons on the left hand side, and the higher ones by those on the right. Wheatstone, Lachenal, and Jeffries were the main producers of Anglos in the past; and Crabbe & Co., and Colin Dipper still produce them in small numbers today.

There is a third type of concertina, known as a 'Duet', for which there are various fingering systems, all attempting to combine the advantages of both main types:- bass on the left, treble on the right; fully chromatic and the same note, push or pull. They have wrist straps like Anglos, and on some, key arrangement makes them look, at first glance, like an Anglo with a large number of buttons. But the 'acid test' is that only an Anglo has two different notes on one button.

Among folk players, those who favour the English system, and those who favour the Anglo are about

The Anglo-Chromatic Concertina

equal in number. The Anglo, with its restriction on keys is not as popular for accompanying songs, although there are those who use it to great effect, notably John Kirkpatrick and the Rev. Kenneth Loveless. The inherent rhythm in the bellows action of the Anglo makes it an ideal instrument to play for ritual or social dance, and the legendary names in this field are the late William Kimber and Scan Tester, both of whom exerted a considerable influence on those who were lucky enough to hear them. The English concertina is not unknown among players for ritual dance, and it is widely used in social dance bands, largely, though not exclusively, as a purely melodic instrument to replace or complement the fiddle. Alistair Anderson of Newcastle has reached a very high degree of virtuosity in this area showing an ability to exploit fully the flowing quality of notes usually associated with the instrument, while instilling it with a seemingly natural sense of rhythm, usually identifiable with the Anglo. Many Irish players use the Anglo for melody without accompaniment and their skill lies in the ability to control the bellows during fast and complex passages so that the Anglo displays the kind of fluid legato quality associated with the English. This smoothness, the ability to play chord in any key, and the soft tone of the English concertina, make it an ideal instrument for the accompaniment of songs. In the early days of the Folk-song Revival, Alf Edwards' accompaniments of A.L. Lloyd, and Peggy Seeger's of Ewan MacColl set a pattern which influenced many followers, and singers such as Louis Killen and Tony Rose have developed styles of self-accompaniment on the instrument.

All this has added up to a great deal of interest in concertinas. Instruments which only a decade or so ago would have been thrown out with the rubbish are now changing hands for very large sums of money. This makes it difficult for the complete

beginner to find an instrument which is both inexpensive and in good pitch and reliable condition. At the height of their production, both Wheatstone and Lachenal produced inexpensive 'tutor' models, with coloured buttons some stamped with the name of the note. Their tone was not as good as their more sophisticated counterparts but they were more than acceptable, and gave encouragement to the learner to keep practising and eventually progress to a better instrument. There are still a number of these in existence, but most are now either quite difficult to find at a reasonable price, or badly in need of attention; and spare parts are difficult to obtain. The new Hohner concertinas are designed also to appeal to the learner. This handbook and fingering chart replace the old coloured and stamped buttons. But the instrument, although not outstanding is certainly adequate, and it is inexpensive and easy to service. It is good news for the beginner that a company with the experience of M.Hohner Ltd., is taking more than a passing interest in the instrument. Such interest is in itself a significant development in the history of the concertina.

Your Hohner Anglo Concertina has 30 playing buttons (the odd one on one side is the air release) . Some concertinas have fewer buttons than this, some more, but an Anglo-Chromatic has its buttons arranged in two, three or four curved rows forward of the wrist strap on each side. Each button operates a lever to lift a pad, so that opening or closing the bellows causes a passage of air to make the reed under that pad vibrate.

If you've played the mouth-organ or the melodeon, you could have a slight advantage when it comes to playing the Anglo, because, like the melodeon, and on the same principle as the harmonica, each button on the Anglo controls *two* notes; one when

Fingering Chart for 30-Key Anglo Concertina

Holding Position, **Anglo concertina**

Left

Right

Air Button

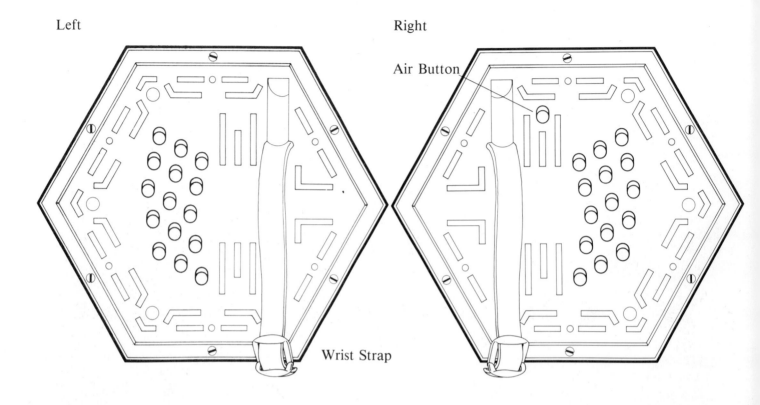

Wrist Strap

The 30-Key Anglo Concertina (Wheatstone System)

	X	C	G		G	C	X	
L5	G♯/B♭	G/A	D/E		G/F♯	C/B	C♯/E♭	R1
L4	A/G	E/F	B/C		B/A	E/D	A/G	R2
L3	C♯/E♭	C/D	G/A		D/C	G/F	G♯/B♭	R3
L2	A/B♭	G/B	D/F♯		G/E	C/A	C♯/E♭	R4
L1	E/F	C/G	B/A		B/F♯	E/B	F/A	R5

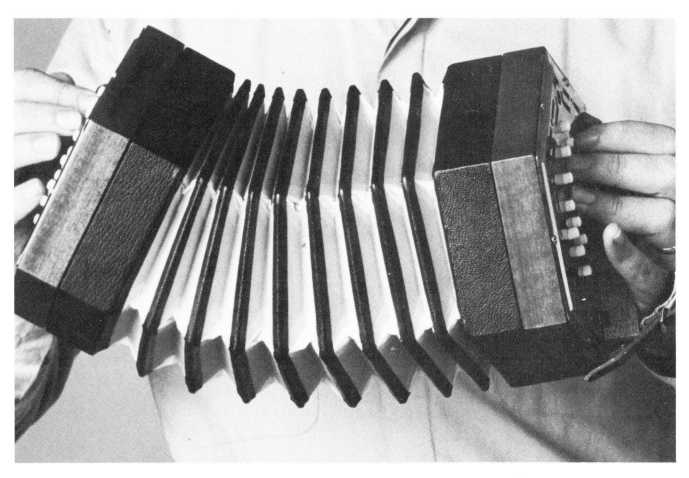

it is blown, and the other when it is sucked, that is, by pushing or pulling the bellows.

Put your hands through the wrist straps, with the exception of your thumbs which go over the tops of the straps. The air button should be on the right hand side, and should be accessible by your thumb. The four fingers of each hand should now be able to reach all the playing buttons on their side. (See illustration for correct holding position.) Adjust the straps so that they are comfortable but not too loose. If you have to spend all your concentration on keeping hold of the instrument because the straps are too slack, you will not be able to play it very well. On the other hand, if you stop the circulation in your fingers, you'll have difficulty using them on the buttons.

It's a good way of discovering muscles you never thought you had, and your thumbs may ache a little at first. Some players prefer to play sitting down and rest one or other end of the concertina on a knee.

For the sake of convenience, let's use a code for the rows and buttons, applicable to the 30-key system of the Hohner, but adaptable to any Anglo. The row nearest to the strap consists of buttons mainly in the key of G, so we'll call it row 'G'. The next one, which does the same for the key of C, can be row 'C'. The remaining one, which is used for various sharps and flats, can be row 'X'. The

buttons on the left hand side on each row, starting from the little finger end, can be respectively **L1**, **L2**, **L3**, **L4** and **L5**, and on the right hand side, starting from the first finger end **R1**, **R2**, **R3**, **R4** and **R5**. There are no hard and fast rules for which fingers control which buttons.

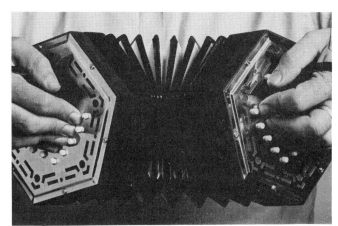

Open the bellows almost to its full extent using the air button. Put the four fingers of your right hand on to the first four buttons of row C; **R1**, **R2**, **R3** and **R4**. Then the four fingers of your left hand on buttons **L2**, **L3**, **L4** and **L5** of row C. Now press the buttons and push the bellows together, and you have a chord of C. So if you push any of these buttons and push the bellows, any other buttons will harmonize with it. Open the bellows again and try the same buttons on row G. A chord of G is what you get.

Use of the Air Button

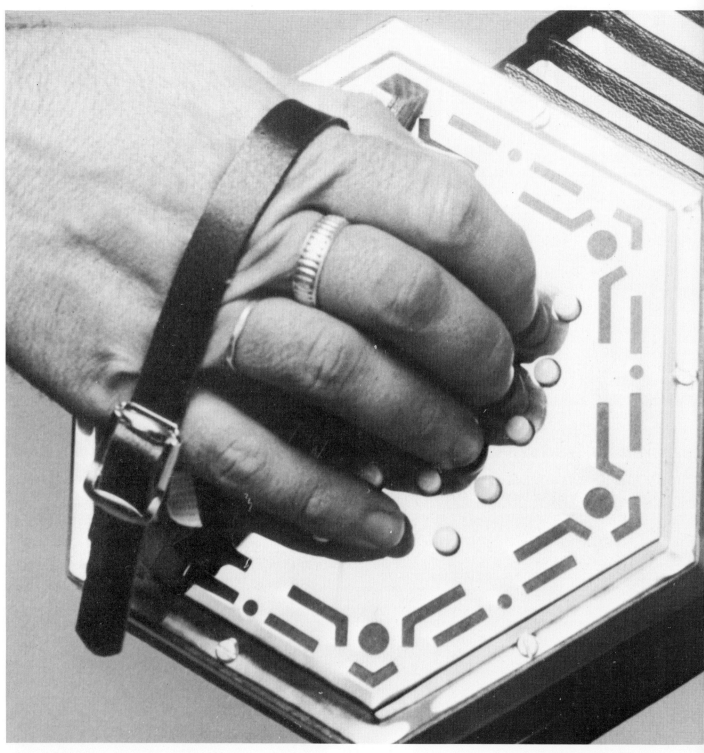

Back on the C row again, cover the buttons **L3**, **L4**, and **L5** with the third, middle and first fingers of your left hand, and button **R1** with the first finger of your right hand. Open the bellows slightly and play the sequence **L3** push, **L3** pull, **L4** push, **L4** pull, **L5** push, **L5** pull, **R1** *pull*, **R1** push. You have just played a scale of C! Do the same on row G, to make a scale of G. Scales are a good way of making yourself familiar with the basic system of the instrument.

Notice while playing these scales that, near the top of each, the normal sequence of push and pull is broken by the two consecutive notes on pull. If you carry on upwards on your right hand, you will find, on either the C row or the G row, that the same occurs at the top of the next scale. The whole score goes:- **R1** push, **R2** pull, **R2** push, **R3** pull, **R3** push, **R4** pull, **R5** *pull*, **R4** *push*.

Now do that without looking at your fingers!

So you're bored with scales now and want to play a real live tune. Try the first one in the selection in the back. You can play it on four buttons of the right hand in either C or G. Don't panic if you've never read music before; the buttons and push/pull instructions are over each note.

The sooner you can develop the confidence to play by feel the better. Once you are sure of your hand position, even the starting note of a tune can be found without looking.

The third row, row X, has several uses. It contains notes which do not fit into the standard keys of C and G, and also notes which occur on the other rows, but on a push instead of a pull or vice versa. This latter feature makes a greater variety of chords available in both keys. Some other keys beside the G and C of the main rows are also possible. At the lower end of the left hand side of row X are the buttons giving most of the notes for a lower scale of C. They are played in conjunction with the lower buttons on row C. In some circumstances, the buttons on row G can be used when playing in C, to give a particular note on the push instead of the pull, or vice versa, or to make an easier fingering sequence for the melody. In the case of the higher reaches of the right hand it can supply notes that are missing from the scale of C on the C row. Likewise, the key of G can be extended downwards by using the C row on the left hand. A glance at the fingering chart and at the buttons used in some of the tunes in the selection in this book will provide examples.

When these buttons are being used, the basic chording principle of 'if it's in the same row and the same direction, it'll harmonize' may break down. For this reason, a number of chord shapes, both push and pull, are shown in the appendix to this section. These are not the only chords possible on the instrument, and they are shown for the left hand only. The more you can work out for yourself, the better.

In fact, as soon as you can appreciate the basic system of the instrument, you should start to work out tunes by ear. The examples given in this book are only suggestions, and intended to show certain principles, which, if developed by the player and applied to his own choice of tunes, will form the basis of an individual style and repertoire.

The air button is used to get air into the instrument if the bellows are too close to play a series of push notes coming up, or too far apart to play a series of pull notes. It can be used at a suitable pause in the melody (as at the end of the first phrase of tune No. 1) or lightly when other buttons are being used to accelerate the opening and closing of the bellows in anticipation of an approaching air shortage or glut. The amount of times you will have to do this depends greatly on how loud or soft you play and how full you choose to make chords; obviously, a chord of three or four notes will use more air than a two-note one. Where alternate fingerings can simplify the bellows action, this is usually indicated in the notes to the tune concerned.

Once you can play this or any of the other simple right hand tunes without having to look at the instructions too often, try 'filling in' on the left hand. Stay on the same row as the melody, and, whatever button or buttons you hit, will make a chord. Trial and error will standardise which buttons make the best chords with which particular notes of the melody, and practice, together with watching other Anglo players will help develop the sense of rhythm for each kind of tune. To make the sound even fuller, try more than one button at a time on the right hand as well. And try all the first few tunes in the back on both rows.
And do it without looking at your fingers!

A Selection of Chords for the Left Hand

Any two or more of the buttons shown in black on the following chord shapes will give chords which may be used to accompany a melody. In this way, music showing guitar chords can be used for the concertina.

A 'vamped' accompaniment can be effected by alternating a low note from a chord with two or more higher ones from the same chord in the required rhythm.

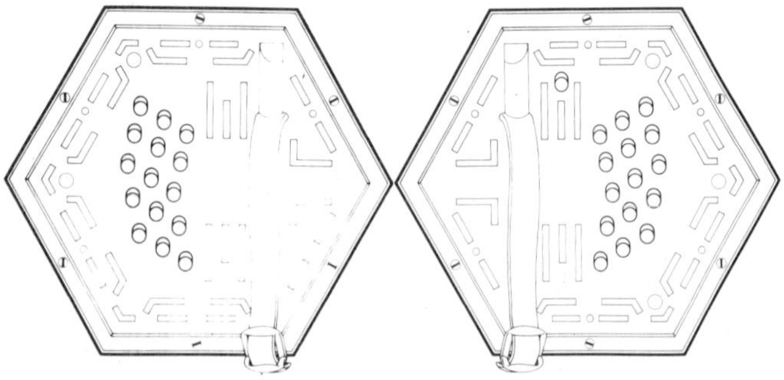

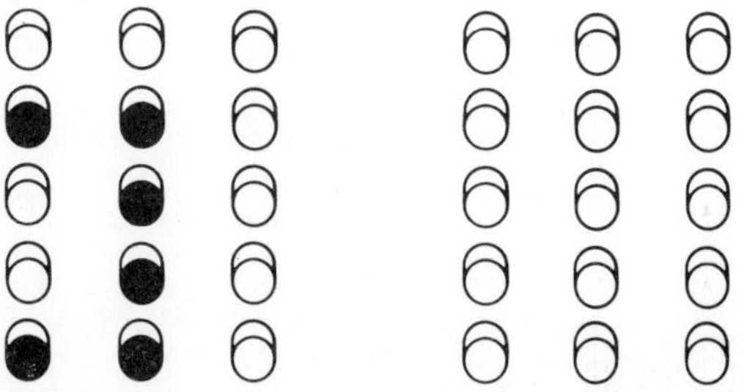

F (PULL)

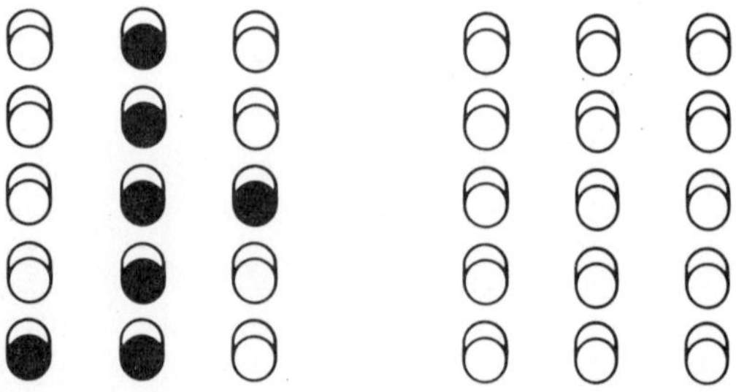

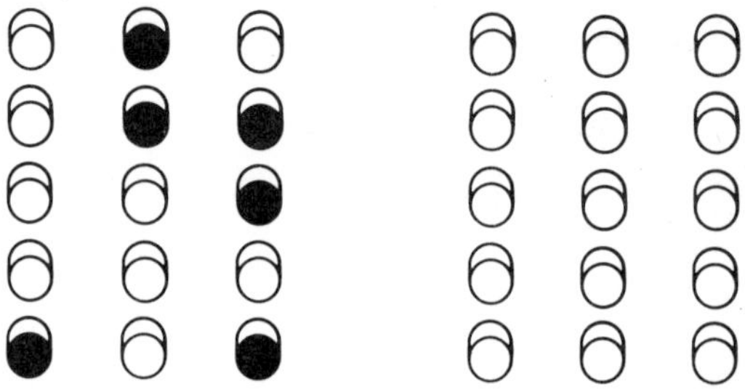

D (PULL)

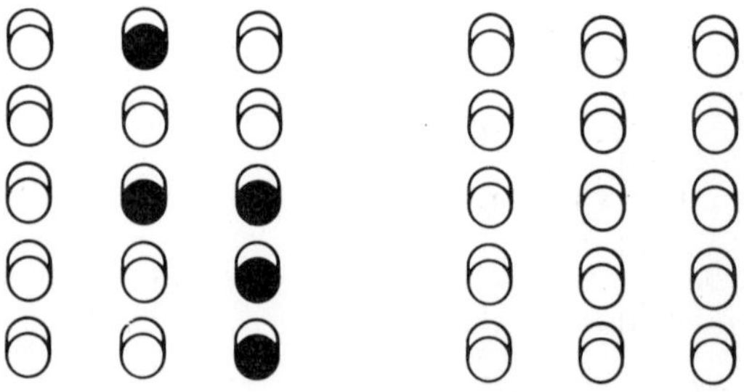

C (PUSH)

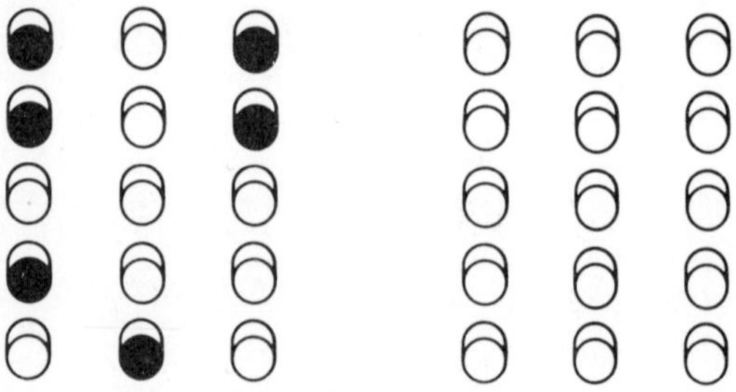

C (PULL)

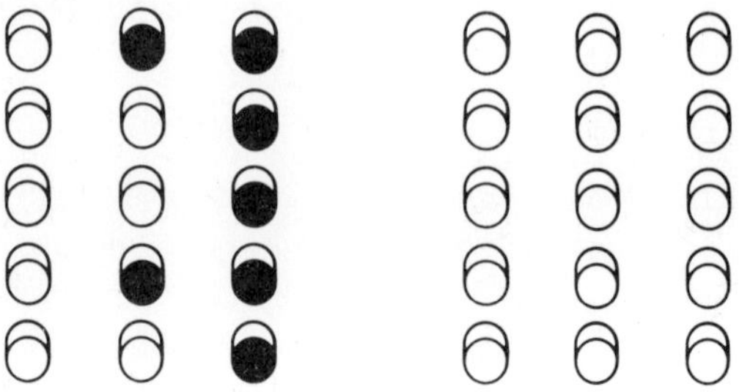

C7 (PULL)

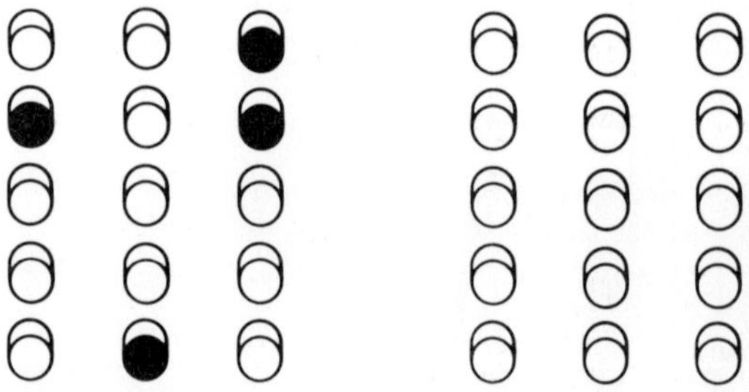

C minor (PULL)

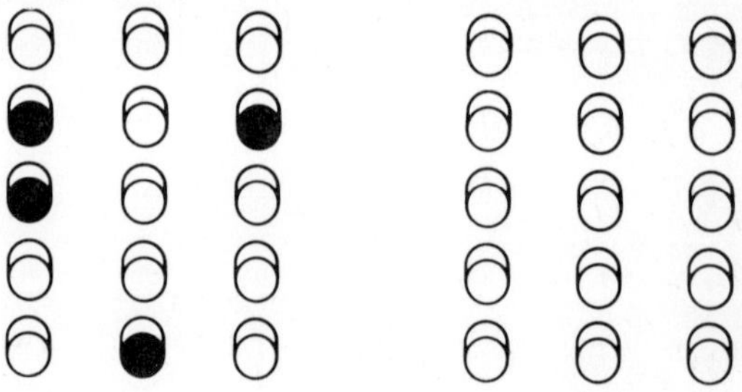

G (PUSH)

G (PULL)

G7 (PULL)

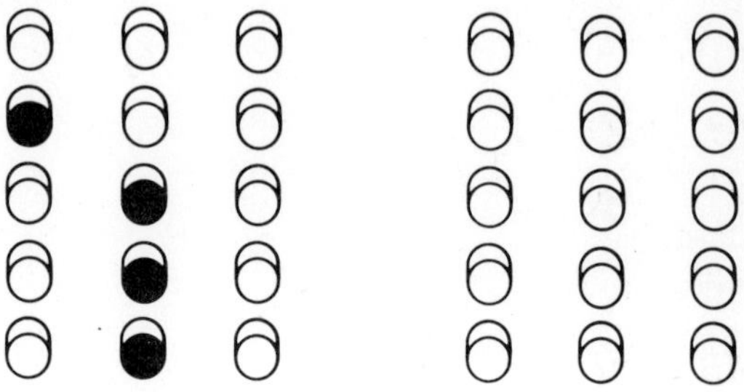

G minor (PULL)

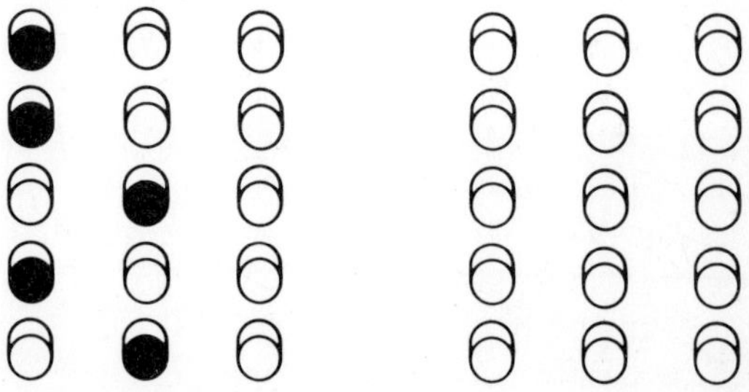

D minor (PULL)

B♭ (PULL)

D7 (PULL)

E minor (PULL)

E minor (PUSH)

E7 (PUSH)

E (PUSH)

A minor (PULL)

A minor (PUSH)

A7 (PUSH)

A (PUSH)

E♭ (PULL)

13

Selection of Folk Tunes

This selection is intended to show various principles which the player can use to build up his or her own repertoire. It is hoped that many of the inclusions will be familiar, so that those whose ability to read music is limited will at least have some idea of how the end-product should sound.

Most of the tunes are popular in musicians' sessions at Folk Festivals. Most festivals include such events as either arranged or informal parts of the programme, and they present an excellent opportunity to practise tunes which you already know and to learn new ones. The atmosphere is encouraging, and the overall sound usually large enough (by virtue of the number of instruments) to

make the occasional mistake irrelevant to all but the person concerned.

For those who envisage the concertina as part of a group line-up, the chords for guitar/banjo/piano are included. These can be used together with the chord diagrams to develop a fuller concertina version of each tune. If a chord is indicated as being played to the whole of a line, this will mean in the case of an Anglo concertina, that, if held on, it would change when the bellows direction changes. Therefore it should be played as often as the bellows are going in the right direction within the rhythm of the tune. Full accompaniments are suggested to the first two tunes to illustrate this.

Monk's March

A Morris dance tune, which can be played on one row, even with a reasonable chorded accompaniment. Take each part separately at first.

Notice the first, second and fourth phrases are the same. Try it on the C row first.

∧ = pull (otherwise push)

Suggested Full Version

*This chord on the pull without a melody note on the
right hand helps to fill the bellows for the section
of push notes which follows.

King Arthur's Servants

A popular song, of which the melody can be played on one row, but with interesting chord shapes if you are prepared to visit the other row occasionally. It is mainly on the G, but the tune can be kept entirely to the right hand if you cross rows for just two notes. The chords can be fuller, as shown in the suggested chorded version, if two rows are used on the left hand.

Practise the melody on one row first, then with the cross on to the other row. When you can play the melody without looking at the instructions too often, try the chords.

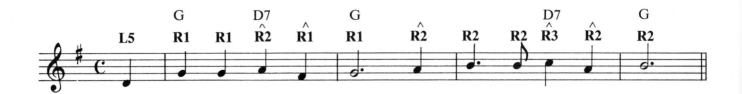

Here are the words to the song:

In good King Arthur's days,
He was a merry king,
He threw three servants out of doors,
Because they would not sing.

CHORUS (to the same tune):
Because they would not sing,
Because they would not sing,
He threw three servants out of doors,
Because they would not sing.

Now, the first was a miller of corn,
And the second was a weaver of yarn,
And the third he was a little tailor,
With the broadcloth under his arm.
       With his broadcloth, etc....

Now the miller, he stole corn,
And the weaver, he stole yarn,
And the little tailor, he stole broadcloth,
To keep those three rogues warm.

The miller was drowned in his dam,
And the weaver was hanged in his yarn,
And the devil put his paw on the little tailor,
With the broadcloth under his arm.

The miller still drowns in his dam,
And the weaver still hangs in his yarn,
And the little tailor, he struts through Hell,
With his broadcloth under his arm.

Suggested Full Version

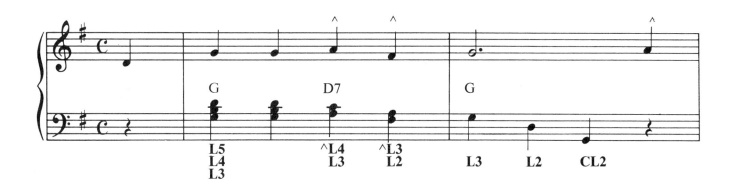

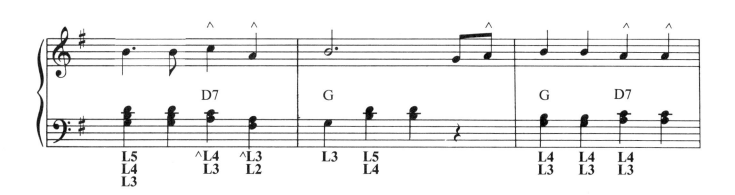

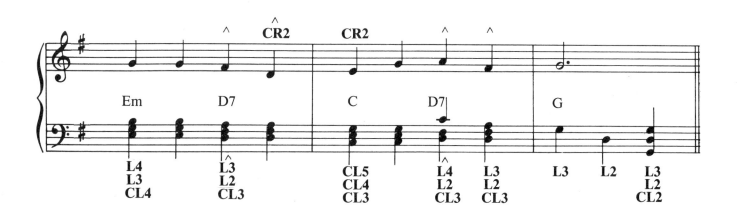

Grandfather's Clock

A tune often played in sessions, more usually as an instrumental than as a song. Again both hands are used, mainly in the third part. But by comparing parts of the tune with cross-rows parts of Tune No.2, and/or looking at the fingering chart, you can keep all or most of it on the right hand, at least in the key of G. (If you want to play it in C you'll have to use both hands).

When you are reasonably confident of the tune in G, look at the chord chart and try to fit some chords to it. The examples already given in full should help you.

Winster Gallop

A country dance tune, with most of the melody on the left hand. This is a style of playing popular in Ireland, and the concertina is used as a lead instrument, chording being more difficult. Try to get the transition between left and right hands as smooth as possible. Try the tune on both rows. (N.B. For the sake of convenience, all tunes, whether played on the right or left hands are written in the treble clef.)

Constant Billy

Another Morris tune. This one explores the upper reaches of the right hand, and again can be played on one, and therefore either row. Written here in G, alternative fingerings as before can keep it all on the right hand for ease of chording.
See 'King Arthur's Servants'.

Star of the County Down

A waltz in a minor key. There are two ways to play minors on the Anglo, one using mainly pull notes and the other with a fair number of pushes in the scale, thus making less use of the air button. The key of A minor can be played in the first way on the G row, and in the second on the C row. Here, alternative fingerings are suggested in some passages to give scope for chording and variation in the bellows action.

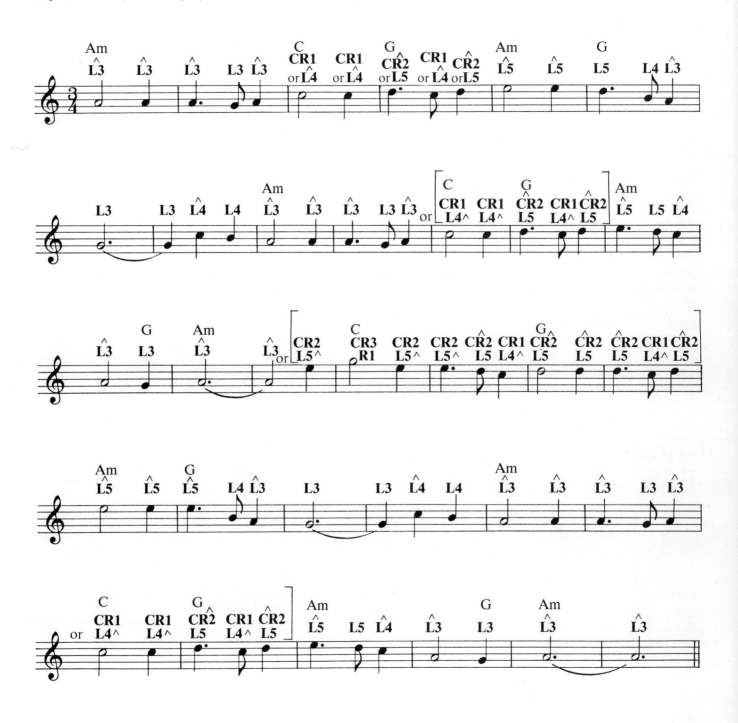

My Love She's But A Lassie Yet

Another dance tune using both hands, and possible
on either row.

Shannon Bells

An Irish jig, using both sides of the concertina,
with a possible cross onto row X, so that some
faster phrases can be kept in the same bellows

direction. Air release time is very limited in a
flowing tune such as this. Go on, indulge yourself
— play it fast!

Double Lead Through

Although written in G, a couple of passages (the B part) of this tune are in D. The key of D uses the note C sharp, and as this is not found on either the C or G rows, we shall have to use row X. Alternative fingerings are given to keep the tune on the right hand, and in one case, using both the C and X rows to keep the bellows in the right direction for the fullest possible A7 chord on the left hand.

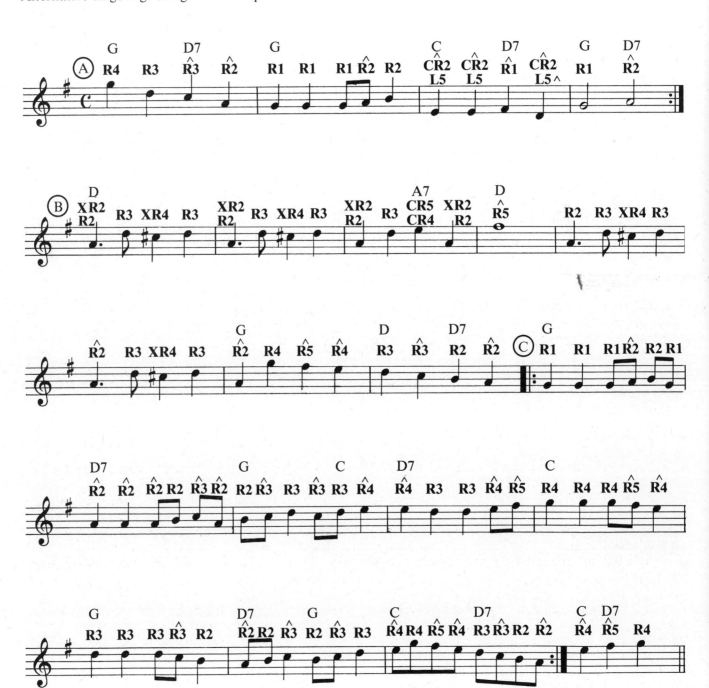

22

Four Drunken Maidens

The key of F is quite feasible on a C/G Anglo,
using mainly the C row with odd visits to row X.
Take some time to practise the melody by itself
before trying chords or words to it.

There were three drunken maidens came from the
Isle of Wight.
They drank from Monday morning, not stopped till
Saturday night,
When Saturday night was come my boys, they
wouldn't then go out,
And these three drunken maidens they pushed the
jug about.

Then in came bouncing Sally, her cheeks as red as
bloom,
'Move up my jovial sisters, and give young Sally
some room.
For I will be your equal, before the night is out.'
And now four drunken maidens, they pushed the
jug about.

There was woodcock and pheasant, and partridge
and hare,
And every kind of dainty; no scarcity was there.
There was forty quarts of ale, my lads, they fairly
drunk it out,
And these four drunken maidens, they pushed the
jug about.

Then in there came the landlord, demanding for his
pay,
A forty pound bill my boys, these girls they had to
pay.
They paid ten pounds apiece my boys, but still they
wouldn't go out,
And these four drunken maidens, they pushed the
jug about.

'Oh where are your feathered hats, your mantles oh
so fine?'
'They've all been swallowed up in tankards of good
wine.'
'And where are your maidenheads, you maidens
brisk and gay?'
'We left 'em in the alehouse, for we drank 'em
clean away.'

Care and Maintenance of the Concertina

The Concertina consists of three major parts, mounted in wooden, or wood and metal ends:— the bellows, the action (buttons, levers and pads) and the reeds.

The bellows may be quite stiff when the instrument is new, but it is wise to avoid putting too much pressure on them to cause them to stretch. They will become easier after a few weeks normal playing. Never force the bellows open or closed without pressing a button (the air release button is provided if you need to open or close the bellows without actually sounding a note; this is likely to happen frequently on the Anglo model), and take care not to stretch the bellows too far; the corners of the bellows could otherwise become slack or damaged, and the screws fixing the bellows to the ends could loosen, causing leakage.

To inspect or service the action or reeds, the ends have to be removed from the bellows. This is done by removing the screws on each side of each end, 6, 8 or 12, depending on how many sides the instrument has. On the Hohner concertina, the reeds are mounted on a separate wooden plate, lodged in the bellows and easily lifted out. The reeds in both cases are grouped in pairs, each pair being controlled by a button. On the English concertina the pairs make the same note; on the Anglo they make different ones. If a reed does not sound, the reason may be that it is impeded by a small foreign body, which can easily be removed. If a reed goes badly out of tune, it should be replaced or tuned by an expert. Service for Hohner concertinas is available from your Hohner dealer. For service for older concertinas, there are a number of tuners and repairers who advertise in the Folk music press.

The most sensitive part of the instrument is the action. To expose the action of a Hohner concertina, remove the end as described above. On the inside, where the reeds are, are two small steel screws; when these are removed, the whole assembly of reeds and action will lift out. With a traditional concertina, the end usually has to be split to expose the action. There are usually two long thin screws, one in the centre of the little finger slide, and one in the centre of the thumb strap mounting on an English, one near the wrist strap bar and one near the buttons on an Anglo. The usual reasons for failure of the action are a broken spring or a loose pad; either of these would result in the note continuing to play when the button is no longer being pressed, — in the case of a broken spring, the button would also stay down. A quick look at the other springs will show how they are mounted. A loose pad is easily re-glued; check that the pad fits snugly over the hole when in position. A small touch of sewing machine oil can be applied to the pivots of the action if necessary,

but care must be taken that there is not enough excess to allow any to be sucked into the reeds when playing.

Most facets of care of the concertina are common sense, and the amount and frequency of maintenance needed are usually directly proportional to the force with which the instrument is regularly played. A musician for a Morris or other ritual dance side, who plays forcefully out in the open air most of the time may find that his reeds need attention more often. A brass reed goes out of tune more quickly than a steel reed; a point to take into consideration when choosing an older instrument.

Early maintenance is best. For this reason it is wise to act on early warning of a reed going out of tune; it can then probably be re-tuned without being weakened; and as you become familiar with the feel of the action, a button with less than the usual resistance will give you early warning that the spring on that lever is getting weak.

And that's about it; except perhaps to point out that a strap into which you have to force your thumb or wrist each time because it is too tight will wear more easily — and however good you are, and however well maintained the reeds, action and bellows, you can't play it if you keep dropping it.

Where To Go From Here

Now the real process of becoming a concertina player begins. Work out your own tunes and song accompaniments by ear or from music. Any book of songs with guitar chords can be used for a start towards working out accompaniments, and for those familiar with them, many written piano ac-companiments can be adapted to the concertina. For dance tunes, the standard collections usually print a melody line only. The more familiar you become with the fingering pattern of the instru-ment, the easier it will be to work things out by ear.

If you meet a key which you have not played before, (many fiddle tunes are written in A, and convenient singing keys vary greatly from person to person), it may be an idea to familiarise yourself with it by playing scales first. Find the note which starts the key on the fingering chart and work up or down in the standard sequence. The number of sharps or flats at the beginning of each line (the 'key signature') will tell you the number of times you will have to use rows 3 or 1x in a scale.